Best-Loved
Chinese Proverbs

Second Edition

ALSO BY THEODORA LAU

The Handbook of Chinese Horoscopes

Chinese Horoscopes for Your Child

The Chinese Horoscopes Guide to Relationships

Best-Loved Chinese Proverbs

Second Edition

THEODORA LAU

WITH KENNETH AND LAURA LAU

COLLINS
An Imprint of HarperCollins Publishers

SECOND EDITION

Designed by Jessica Shatan Heslin/Studio Shatan, Inc.

ISBN 978-0-06-170365-2

This book is dedicated to our family,
whose love and support are beyond compare.

Contents

Contents

Contents

Contents

Introduction

The first edition of *Best-Loved Chinese Proverbs* was published in 1995. In our second edition, we have added some new interpretations of Chinese proverbs. We have enjoyed hearing from our readers how these proverbs have provided inspiration, comfort, and a new avenue of communication in life's trials and blessings. The appeal of Chinese proverbs has always been profound and universal. The beauty of these statements is in their brevity and simplicity. Their mission to give a direct message that will reach the heart and mind of the reader is often achieved with aplomb and finesse.

These down-to-earth and succinct compositions summarize and crystallize the penetrating wit and wisdom of the Han people for the benefit of all. Like intense beams of light, these proverbs highlight truths in life that are evident but often ignored or unrealized.

The Chinese proverbs here were derived indirectly from old Chinese texts. Being interpreted in English not only brings out their timeless value but gives new dimensions in expression. These well-tested truths of condensed knowledge can once again be used to observe and to instruct.

Most of the proverbs here are poetically expressed in the words of the author. They are original verse, not verbatim translations of any Chinese text. Some are not even translations at all but are distillations of several sayings from different sources. Because of the antiquity of these sayings, all have unknown origins. Different regions of China may also have different versions. But as they say, to truly know a people, know their proverbs.

It is our belief that the value of Chinese proverbs has only increased with the passing of the ages: they ring as true today as they have for thousands of years. We have retrieved, molded, and polished these proverbs to introduce them in a new and revealing light. We hope that you will enjoy this new edition of them as much as we loved writing them for you.

— Theodora, Kenneth, and Laura Lau

A Word about
Chinese Calligraphy

BY KENNETH LAU

All the Chinese calligraphy here is in the proper unabbreviated form of original and traditional Chinese, not the simplified version commonly used in China today. This traditional form of calligraphy is followed in Hong Kong, Taiwan, and Singapore and is an important part of Chinese culture.

All the words have auspicious meanings and are meant to be positive, uplifting, or inspiring. Chinese characters denoting negative or inauspicious meanings are generally not exhibited, as their influence is considered unlucky and unhappy for people.

There are about five thousand Chinese characters or words commonly used in the language; when these are combined, they produce a rich and powerful vocabulary of new words and usage with thousands of possibilities. Sometimes a single character will suffice—as in the words "love," "endurance," "fortune," and "livelihood"—but in most instances compound characters are used to clarify, emphasize, and deepen the meaning. Compound characters eliminate any possibility of confusion, double meaning, or misinterpretation, for written Chinese is precise in expression.

Chinese is a pictorial language based on drawn symbols rather than on sound, as you can see on the following pages. Words are classified according to their "radical" or root and are located under their corresponding class. If one is looking in a Chinese dictionary for a word related to water, such as "juice," "river," "stream," or "rain," one will find all these words having the common sign of water (shuǐ: 水) (radical: 氵) preceding the Chinese character and incorporated into the written form for that word. Likewise, emotions will all have the sign for heart (xīn: 心) contained in their written form to describe where the word is derived from.

Pronunciation Key

The pronunciation key given here is based on the modern Chinese phonetic alphabet.

Ability	jì	技	skill, trick
	néng	能	energy, ability
Admiration	xiàn	羡	envy, jealousy
	mù	慕	admiration, praise
Cooperation	xié	協	jointly, three symbols of strength 力
	zhù	助	help, combined effort

Courtesy	lǐ	禮	etiquette, salute, rite, ceremony
	mào	貌	appearance, proper manners
Diligence	qín	勤	single-mindedness, industriousness
	fèn	奮	vigorous exertion
Foresight	yuǎn	遠	extensiveness
	xièn	見	sight, vision
Fortune	fú	福	wealth, happiness, good prospects, and the ability to enjoy these blessings
Happiness	xǐ	禧	jubilation, joy, felicity, auspiciousness

Honor	róng	榮	flourish, abundance
	yù	譽	fame, reputation, renown
Inspiration	gǔ	鼓	encouragement, incitement
	wǔ	舞	dance
Knowledge	zhī	知	understanding
	shí	識	recognition
Livelihood	shēng	生	birth, growth, procreation
	huó	活	live, alive
Longevity	shòu	壽	long life, continuity
Love	aì	愛	emotion coming from the center of the heart

Morality	daò	道	road, way, path
	dé	德	virtue, ethics
Opportunity	jī	機	chance, opportunity
	huì	會	ability, meet, a moment
Patience	nài	耐	endurance
	xīn	心	the heart
Perseverance	rěn	忍	bear, endurance, a knife above the heart
Profit	lì	利	benefit, advantage
	rùn	潤	flow, lubrication, smoothness
Sincerity	chéng	誠	honesty, sincerity
	yì	意	intention, idea, meaning
Strategy	cè	策	a plan, a scheme
	lüè	略	a strategy

Success	chéng	成	accomplishment, acquisition
	gōng	功	merit, achievement, skill
Superiority	yōu	優	dominance, preponderance
	shì	勢	position
Victory	shèng	勝	success
	lì	利	strength
Wealth	cái	財	abundance, rich
	fù	富	money
Wisdom	zhì	智	wit, wisdom
	huì	慧	brightness, perception, intelligence

技能

劉克昌

Ability

Ability

Ability in itself is nothing when
denied opportunity.

~

Anyone can sail a ship when the sea is calm.

~

Judge a person not by his ability to make money,
but by his ability to retain it.

~

Control the winds by trimming your sails.

*Focus your efforts on honing your talents, and you will
be better prepared to face uncertainty.*

~

Limitations are but boundaries created inside
our minds.

~

Only time and effort bring proficiency.

~

First attain skill; creativity comes later.

~

The wind and the waves seem always to favor the best sailors.

Those with true skill know how to make opportunities in any environment.

Adaptability

Clumsy birds have need of early flight.

*Those with less ability should work harder instead
of making excuses.*

~

An old broom has its value.

*One should value previous contacts and avoid discarding old friends
or people who have helped you before.*

~

Make the cap fit the head.

Know where and when to make adjustments.

~

Better to bend in the wind than to break.

~

When the wind is great, bow before it; when
the rain is heavy, yield to it.

~

Any garment will fit one who is naked.

*One must adapt to circumstances, just as water
must take the shape of its container.*

~

A young branch takes all the bends one gives it.

The young can adapt to change with great ease.

~

Fashion is a tyrant who dictates
never-ending changes.

美慕

劉克昌

Admiration

Admiration

One whose breath is felt in heaven.

Denotes a person of great consequence and importance.

~

The best form of flattery is to master the
art of listening.

~

No matter how tall the mountain, it cannot block
out the sun.

*A common saying of parents who idolize their offspring and liken
the child's abilities to the sun.*

Adversity

Adversity is a mirror that reveals one's true self.

~

Adversity brings us into deep waters not to drown us, but to cleanse us.

~

One who has never met adversity will not develop foresight.

~

Unless there is opposing wind, a kite cannot rise.

Opposition and adversity give us a chance to rise to new heights.

~

Adversity teaches us life's most valuable lessons.

Challenges are the most truthful and strictest of teachers.

~

Jade is shaped to become a valuable tool.

*All great minds become valuable through the
lessons of time and experience.*

~

Those who know the storm dread the calm
before it.

~

Do not give nuts to those who have no teeth.

*Give challenges to those who have the character
to face them.*

~

Trials are blessings in disguise.

Anger

To eat the wind and swallow bitterness.

*An expression referring to one who harbors resentment, represses
anger, and endures suffering.*

~

To have one's liver on fire.

*Anger is said to originate from the liver, so this
expression is used when a person is extremely angry.*

~

To stir the fire and burn oneself.

This means to bring trouble upon oneself through anger.

~

Harsh words and poor reasoning never
settle anything.

~

Do not create in anger what you lack
in reason.

~

In anger, a person becomes a danger to himself
and to others.

~

Do not upset heaven and earth.

*An expression to calm someone who is creating a disturbance or
having an outburst of anger.*

~

If you control yourself in one moment of
anger, you will escape a hundred days of sorrow.

~

Anger is a luxury one cannot afford.

~

Love, anger, and money betray themselves.

~

It is wiser to vent anger than to contain it.

Beauty

That which is beautiful is not always good.
But that which is good is always beautiful.

~

True beauty is eternal and cannot be destroyed.

~

One who seeks beauty with a pure heart
finds what he is searching for.

Caution

The cautious seldom err.

~

An overturned cart ahead warns the one behind.

*A keen observer is the mark of a great student. Learn
from those who have come before you.*

~

Don't jump over a pit only to fall into a well.

~

Be slow to promise but quick to perform.

~

Better to be too skeptical than to be too trusting.

~

Presumptions will bring nothing but trouble.

~

Uncertainty breeds caution.

~

When fortune flirts, her smile is costly.

Be cautious when presented with promised windfalls that require little investment.

~

A loan is like rice eaten. It is soon forgotten.

Man's memory can be altered when in a situation of urgent need. Make loans cautiously.

~

It is cheaper to give a small sum than to lend a large amount.

~

A wolf may lose its fangs, but not its inclinations.

Character

There is no poverty where there is character, and
no wealth or honor where character is missing.

~

One who has character has courage.

~

Fortunes may rise and fall and kingdoms may
tumble, but one's character never changes.

True change in a person is very rare.

~

Where there is character, ugliness becomes
beauty; where there is no character,
beauty becomes ugliness.

Compromise

One who would pick the roses must bear with
the thorns.

*One learns compromise by accepting the good
with the bad.*

~

Compromise is always a temporary achievement.

*When compromise turns into commitment,
it becomes permanent.*

~

One who learns the value of compromise
acquires wisdom.

Conflict

Those who are unable to live under the same sky.

A common saying to denote bitter enemies who cannot coexist.

~

A long journey tests a horse; a long-drawn-out conflict tests a friendship.

~

Settle a small conflict quickly and you will keep a hundred others at bay.

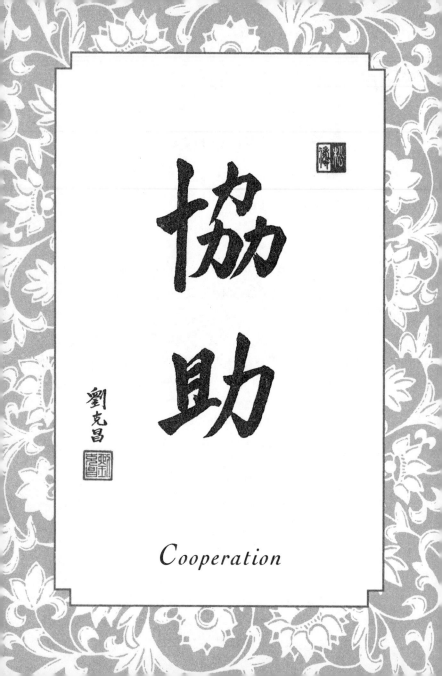

協助

劉克昌

Cooperation

Cooperation

Strength + strength + strength = cooperation

The Chinese word for "cooperation" is composed of the symbol for strength repeated three times. A heart radical is also present to symbolize the common intention necessary to achieve synergy.

~

A single tree cannot make a forest. A single beam cannot support a great house.

~

Refusal to cooperate with evil is equal to cooperating with good.

~

What is good for the hive is good for the bee.

~

One sings, all follow.

An expression that means everyone is in agreement.

~

A cloth is not woven from a single thread.

~

A bridge is not built from one piece of wood.

~

We cannot clap with only one hand.

~

Each person equals a grain of sand, but an
army is like a block of gold.

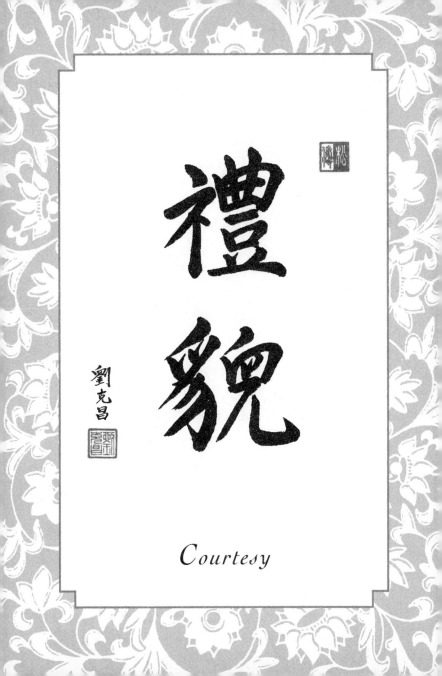

禮貌

劉克昌

Courtesy

Courtesy

Courtesy is the mark of a civilized person.

~

Kindness is the best quality of the soul.

~

Follow the good and learn their ways.

~

Keeping company with the wicked is like
living in a fish market: one becomes
used to the foul odor.

People adapt to their environment,
for better or worse.

~

Kind words can be brief and simple, yet
they echo in our memories forever.

~

It is difficult to forgive those who steal our time.

~

The insolent are often the wounded.

The courteous learn manners from those who have none.

Crisis

The Chinese word for "crisis" is the character for
danger in front of the character for opportunity.

*This means that a crisis brings both danger
and opportunity.*

~

No sooner has one pushed a gourd under water
than another pops up.

*A common saying that describes having one
crisis after another.*

~

One who does not burn incense when all is well,
but clasps Buddha's feet when in trouble.

*An expression used to describe someone who
calls on you only when in a crisis.*

Criticism

Criticism must be used lightly. A gentle wind
kindles, while a strong wind kills the fire.

~

One who hears flattery, but not criticism,
will go astray.

~

The one who snores the loudest will fall asleep first.

One who criticizes is often oblivious to his own faults.

~

One who blows fur to find the scar underneath.

*Used of a person who loves to find fault and will look
in the most hidden places to uncover flaws.*

~

Those who need advice most will accept it least.

~

Only the wearer knows where the shoe pinches.

*Some situations are not open for criticism. There are
times when only those intimately involved know
where to improve.*

~

Good advice is like bitter medicine.

~

Opening a wound to treat it could create
a new injury.

Deception

Beware of one with a honeyed tongue and
a sword in the belly.

*A known enemy is dangerous, but a false
friend is worse.*

~

Don't be a tiger's head with a snake's tail.

*A strange combination used to describe someone who
presents an important front with no substance
behind it.*

~

Do not increase the size of your face by
beating your cheeks swollen.

*A proverb used to describe those who, trying to
impress others, puff themselves up.*

~

If the top beam is crooked, all the rest
will not be straight.

*A saying used to refer to corruption or bribery
in government or large companies.*

~

Deception is often not worth the price one pays.

~

One becomes double-minded from
suspicion and guilt.

Deceptive people find it difficult to believe others.

~

A paper tiger cannot bear close scrutiny.

*This means that the threat is frightening only from a
distance; it is ineffective when viewed up close.*

~

He who digs a hole for another
may fall in himself.

~

Do not be outwardly a fierce bull but
inwardly as timid as a mouse.

~

One who is as disappointing as an
empty dumpling.

*This is used of someone who makes empty
promises or fails to live up to expectations.*

~

Do not be caught with dye on the fingers.

*A warning to those who might be caught
stealing or taking a bribe.*

Defeat

Defeat teaches us life's most valuable lessons.

~

Defeat is never a bitter brew until one agrees to swallow it.

Defeat is never final unless we accept it.

~

To be unhappy over what one lacks is to waste what one already possesses.

~

Avoid defeat and you will avoid success.

~

A tiny leak will eventually sink a mighty ship.

Defeat is often the result of a lack of foresight.

~

An error the width of a hair can lead one a thousand miles astray.

Small errors can lead to defeat. Focusing on the details can keep one on course.

~

A drowning person will not be troubled by a little rain.

勤

奮

劉克昌

Diligence

Diligence

Do not hope to reach a destination without ever leaving the shore.

~

Diligence and constancy of purpose achieve the impossible.

~

A man of leisure will never taste the fruit of success.

~

To chop a tree quickly, spend twice the time sharpening your ax.

Discretion

One who is tripped by the foot can get up again.
One who is tripped by the tongue may not.

~

Think before you speak, and do not speak
all that you think.

~

Mastering discretion is greater than employing
eloquence.

*Knowing when to speak is more important than
being an eloquent speaker.*

~

Discretion is more precious than great learning.

~

Be just to all, but trust not all.

~

For the love of money, truth falls silent.

Silence as well as discretion can be bought.

~

Silence condemns more effectively than loud accusations do.

~

If the arm is broken, hide it in the sleeve.

One should not display dirty linens in public.

~

To rise high, conceal ambition.

~

Nothing is as heavy as a secret.

Falsehood/Gossip

Even the powerful ox has no defense against flies.

~

An idle story can quickly become fact in the mouths of hundreds.

~

Good deeds never leave home; bad ones echo for a thousand miles.

Unfortunately, our worst moments garner the most discussion.

~

When the tongue slips, it speaks the truth.

~

One who mounts a tiger can never get off.

Once you enter politics, it is difficult to exit.

~

The larger one's roof, the more snow
it will collect.

*One of the prices of prosperity is the difficult
job of managing one's reputation.*

~

True words may not be pleasant; pleasant
words may not be true.

*Compliments are easier to give than criticism —
ponder both.*

~

Hearing about something one hundred
times is not worth seeing it once.

~

Do not judge matters from a single occurrence.

~

A tongue is the only instrument that grows
sharper with constant use.

~

Two hands should be twice as busy
as one tongue.

~

Shovel the snow only from your own
doorstep. Do not mind the frost forming
on your neighbor's roof.

~

Do not lay a corpse at someone else's door.

*Do not drag others into troubles that
do not concern them.*

~

Truth must take the straight road,
while lies travel on the wind.

Family/Home

The state of the nation is reflected in the home.

If each home is strong, so will the country be.

~

Once one is a teacher, one becomes a
parent for life.

*The Chinese believe that the responsibility of a
teacher is the same as that of a parent.*

~

Govern a family as you would fry a small fish:
very, very carefully.

~

Wherever one finds comfort can be
called home.

~

The lamb kneels to suckle.

*A favorite expression describing filial piety,
gratitude, and respect for one's parents.*

~

A pearl from an old oyster.

*A saying about a precious offspring born to someone
who is almost past childbearing age.*

~

If one is in harmony with his family, he has found
the secret of success.

~

Better a hundred foes outside the home than one
enemy within.

~

One generation plants the trees for the next
generation to enjoy the shade.

Fate

Man can cure a multitude of illnesses,
but not fate.

~

What is fated to be yours will always return
to you.

~

Often one finds destiny just where one hides to
avoid it.

~

Extremes will meet. Everything will have a
beginning and an end.

~

Fate is influenced by good deeds.

*It is said that the good deeds of one generation
can influence the fate of the next. If one in need is helped
by a good Samaritan, another may observe,
"Your parents must have been very kind to others to
have paved your path so smooth."*

~

A bridge never crossed is like a life never lived.

~

Fate leads those who are willing but must push
those who are not.

~

A person's character will determine his destiny.

Fire

Fire does not produce fire. Eventually it reduces all to ashes.

One should not overwork or burden himself.

~

A great fire may follow a tiny spark.

A simple idea can move a people.

~

Do not set fire to the forest to drive out the wolves.

Sometimes drastic measures, although effective, are not practical.

遠見

劉克昌

Foresight

Foresight

One who refuses to look ahead will remain behind.

~

Weaving a net is better than praying for fish at the edge of the water.

~

Bend one cubit, make eight cubits straight.

Correcting a problem early prevents more down the road.

~

Do not build what is permanent upon the sand.

Be sure to have a firm foundation before wasting time, effort, and money in any endeavor.

~

First resolve what must be done; solutions will then become evident.

~

One must cut before filing, carve before polishing.

~

Remember to dig the well long before you get thirsty.

~

If one takes no thought about what is distant, he will find sorrow near at hand.

~

Do not hasten to rejoice at someone's departure until you see his replacement.

~

To avoid misunderstanding, start small.

Communicate early and often when working on a complicated project.

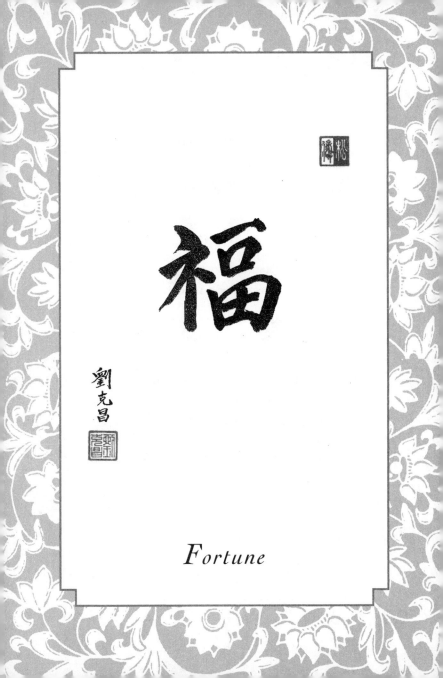

福

劉克昌

Fortune

Fortune

What first appears as a calamity may later
bring good fortune.

*Fortune may surprise you — do not be quick to
quit a difficult situation.*

~

The tide must reach its lowest before it turns.

~

Look to your enemy for a chance to succeed.

*Observe your opponent and you will find new
ways to succeed.*

~

Every day cannot be a feast of lanterns.

Everyone will know both joy and sorrow.

~

Fortune comes in many disguises.

~

No one stays atop the wheel of fortune
all the time.

*Because the wheel of fortune brings ups and downs
to everyone in life, the hope is that it will slow for you
to enjoy the good times and spin quickly during
the challenges.*

~

Earth is to the dead what gold is to the living.

*The living and dead have different needs. This
saying alludes to a reversal of fortune.*

~

He who has no coin has no power.

~

To have wealth enough to have your mill run
by a ghost.

Money can buy almost anything.

~

Great fortunes need luck; small ones depend on
diligence.

~

Fortune has a fickle heart and a short memory.

~

Be as fortunate as one who rests on high pillows.

A wish for someone to feel as fortunate as one who lives an elevated life of ease and luxury without any worries.

~

When luck visits you, everyone will know where you live.

Frugality/Prosperity

Frugality is the mother of prosperity.

~

Economize now or suffer want later.

~

Be frugal in prosperity, fear not in adversity.

Store and save for that rainy day.

~

Prosperity brings us friends; adversity
drives them away.

~

One must be just before one is generous.

~

The wise make good use of prosperity.

~

The hand that gives is greater than the
hand that takes.

A miser is condemned to be forever in want.

~

Hunger is a great teacher.

~

Frugality makes one independent.

Futility

When the itch is inside the boot, scratching
outside provides little consolation.

*This proverb expresses the futility of not being
able to deal directly with a problem.*

~

Don't try to scoop the moon from the bottom
of the sea.

Deal with problems directly, rather than from afar.

~

A Buddha made of mud crossing a river cannot protect himself.

The Buddha symbolizes one who is powerful, but in a vulnerable situation he is powerless to take care of himself. Therefore, it is pointless to expect the Buddha to assist us under such conditions.

~

Do not draw a snake and add feet to it.

This expression is used to describe the point at which no improvements are needed.

~

One does not light a candle to challenge the sun.

~

To see another's dust but be unable to overtake him.

Know when you have been bested.

~

Wherever there is iron, there is also rust.

Greed

Water quenches thirst and food sates our hunger,
but no amount of gold will satisfy greed.

~

Do not learn to desire what you do not deserve.

~

Do not gather together like ants.

*Ants are likened to greedy thieves and signify those who
benefit from the misery of others.*

~

Money can turn a lowly worm into a mighty
dragon.

~

Do not have eyes that are bigger than your stomach.

This is a common saying from parents to children, admonishing those who take more food than they can eat.

~

Our needs are few, but our wants increase with our possessions.

Greed feeds upon itself.

~

Greed comes into one's heart to steal peace of mind.

~

One who marries for money must eventually earn it.

~

There is no greater calamity than being consumed by greed.

~

Lust and greed have no limit.

~

Fat fries and burns itself.

This saying is used to describe greedy and powerful people who are usually the instruments of their own destruction.

~

One who does not receive just wages will seek to pay himself.

~

Be the master of your money, not its slave.

~

To buy a quarrel, lend money to a friend.

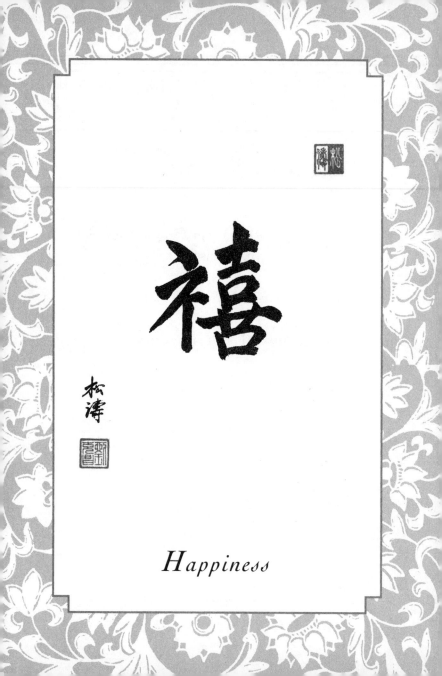

禧

松濤

Happiness

Happiness

A happy person is one not trapped by fame and fortune.

~

With happiness comes wisdom into the heart.

~

It is wealth enough to learn the meaning of contentment.

Happy hearts are rich in so many ways.

~

Happiness is when we finally become what we have always wished to be.

~

To live well is better than to be rich.

Harmony/Contentment

Solitude is enjoyed only when one is at
peace with oneself.

*One who has a guilty conscience finds it hard to
enjoy his own company.*

~

When you drink of the spring be thankful
for the source.

*Know where your blessings come from and do not
forget to give thanks to those who helped you.*

~

Those who seek harmony know how to find it.

~

Laughter is the music of one's soul. One is never
really poor if he can afford to laugh.

~

We earn a living by what we do, but we make
a life by what we give.

~

It is better to like what you have than to have
what you like.

~

He who loves music learns to soothe his
own sorrows.

Heart

To use with a small heart.

*This saying means to use something with caution
or handle with extreme care.*

~

To have a thin heart.

*This is used to describe a very cautious person —
a perfectionist.*

~

To treat others with a thick heart.

This refers to someone who is careless or clumsy.

~

To care for the heart.

This means to empathize with others.

~

Do not waste your heart.

To waste your heart is to waste your time.

~

To have a black heart.

A strong statement in Chinese culture; refers to an evil person.

~

Sorrowing hearts are always unsettled.

~

Forgiveness is an act of the heart.

"Forgiveness" is written in Chinese with the word for "act" or "compliance" above the symbol for the heart.

~

Put your heart at rest.

Calm yourself and quiet your worries.

~

There is no cure for hidden grief.

Conceal your sorrow and you will find no remedy.

~

Wishes of mind and heart are as hard to control
as a horse and an ape.

*This means that one's mental and emotional wishes
are in conflict and pulling in separate directions.*

~

A calm heart adjusts to many changes.

~

To accommodate all things, enlarge your heart.

A generous heart knows no bounds.

~

Gratitude is an act of a good heart.

~

Music cheers the heart and warms the disposition.

~

A kind person's mouth is found in the heart.

*A compassionate person will speak through thoughtful
acts rather than just saying the right things to
impress others.*

~

Good heart, good reward.

A just heart has its own rewards.

~

Flowers are known by the fruit they bear.

One who follows nature will never lose his way.

~

The worst prison is one made of the heart.

*One who cannot or will not permit oneself to
love is one's own jailer.*

~

We can find no wealth above a healthy body
and a happy heart.

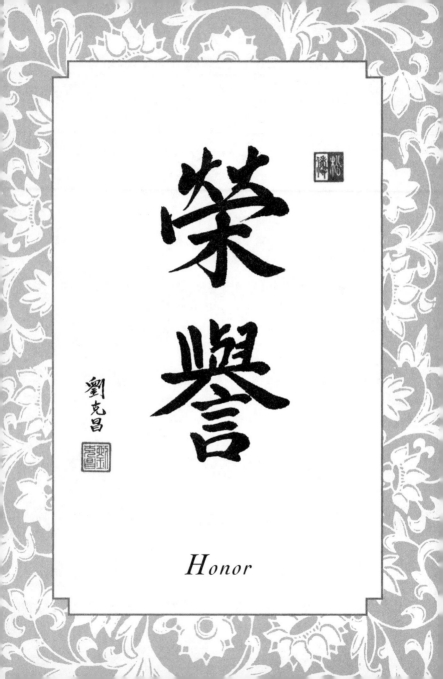

荣誉

劉克昌

Honor

Honor

A noble ancestry cannot guarantee a noble character.

~

When a leopard dies, he leaves his coat. When a man dies, he leaves his name.

Your legacy will live forever.

~

An honorable person is a majority of one.

~

A clear conscience is the greatest armor.

~

Virtue travels uphill, vice travels downhill.

~

Life and shame are never equal to death and glory.

~

He who must pursue glory may sacrifice honor.

~

Shed the bones, change the face.

To be reborn and start anew.

~

To lose the glow of one's face.

To suddenly lose one's reputation or credibility.

~

A man must despise himself before others will.

~

Great eloquence cannot change
wrong into right.

Horses

Be on a horse when you go in search of a better one.

An admonition that one should be cautious when trading up in life. It is always easier to replace something new while you still have the old as a backup.

~

He wants to buy the best horse: one that does not eat grass.

This proverb describes someone who is too calculating, unrealistic, and never satisfied. This person wants something for nothing or wishes for something that does not exist, like a horse that does not eat grass.

~

The old horse will know the way.

~

A clever horse needs only one touch of the whip.

Someone who is intelligent and astute needs only one little hint to understand the situation.

~

Rein in the horse at the edge of the cliff.

Pull oneself back at the last moment and stop before plunging over the precipice.

~

Do not doctor a dead horse as if it were alive.

Humility

More demands on oneself and few demands on others will keep resentment at bay.

~

The superior man does not think himself so. His humility is what sets him apart.

~

It's something not worth hanging on the teeth.

A polite response that reflects humility when someone thanks you for a favor. This proverb uses exaggeration to minimize the importance of the service by saying that it was so inconsequential that it could not even pass between the teeth.

~

He who speaks without modesty will not keep his promises.

~

Little persons try to be perfect, while great ones do not know they are great.

~

A burnt tongue becomes shy of hot soup.

Mistakes make one timid.

Indecision

The wise make their own decisions.
The ignorant follow public opinion.

~

Indecisiveness breeds confusion.

~

Do not have each foot on a different boat.

Choose a direction and do not look back.

~

One whose heart is not content cannot
make good decisions.

~

Reticence builds a fortress in the mind.

One who is unsure or fearful puts up mental barriers.

~

To draw the bow but not release the arrow.

To make threats without following through with positive action or a decision.

~

Indecision hinders luck and fortune.

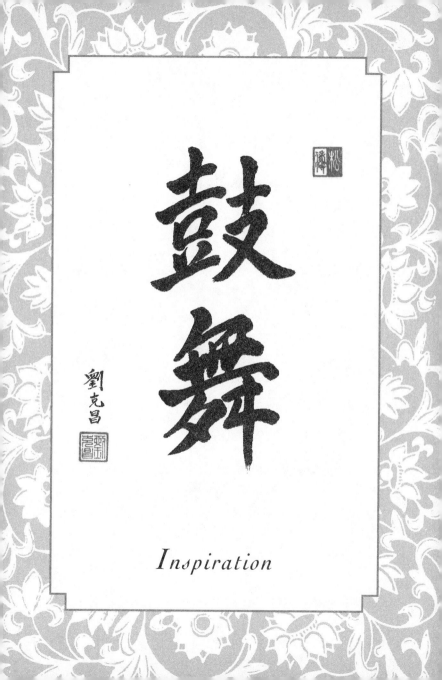

鼓舞

Inspiration

Inspiration

Cowards have dreams; brave men have visions.

~

One's merits should not be a hindrance
to one's progress.

~

Review past lessons to discover anew.

*Old lessons read with a new perspective can bring about new
interpretations.*

~

Do not skim the surface like the dragonfly
kisses the water.

*The dragonfly merely glides over a pond. Search
for deep meaning.*

~

The darker the night, the brighter the stars.

~

Learning is like the horizon: there is no limit.

~

With experience, we will gain full knowledge.
Inspiration will follow.

~

To feel the catch of the lock.

*This expression is used to describe one is who able to
comprehend the key to the situation, the crux of the
matter, or the most important point in a discussion.*

~

A goal without a deadline is only a wish.
A dream with a deadline becomes a goal.

~

Ideas enlarge the mind and never allow it to go
back to its original dimension.

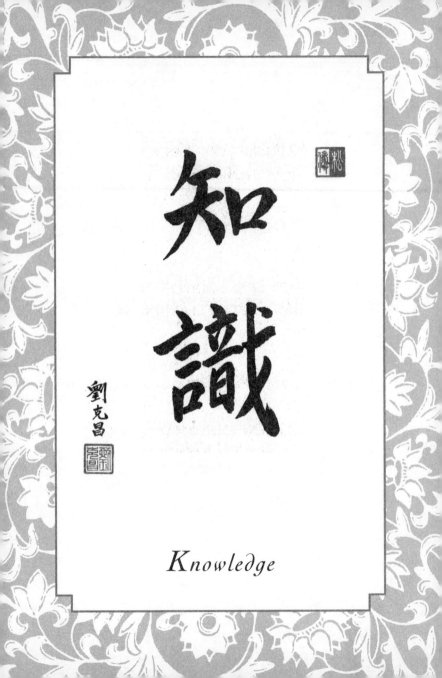

知

識

劉克昌

Knowledge

Knowledge

By filling one's head instead of one's pocket,
one cannot be robbed.

An education can never be stolen.

~

Common sense goes further than much learning.

~

Despise learning and make everyone pay for
your ignorance.

*Ignorance or illiteracy is an expense that society as
a whole must bear.*

~

If you are planning for a year, plant rice.
If you are planning for a decade, plant trees.
If you are planning for a lifetime, educate people.

~

One who does not like to read is equal to one who
cannot read.

~

A night without moon or stars is like an ignorant
mind.

~

More powerful than any army is an idea whose
time has arrived.

~

A frequent path will become a road.

~

Wheat stalks heavy with grain learn how to bow
their heads.

*Matured stalks symbolize learned and humble persons
who acknowledge that they do not know everything,
while empty-headed young stalks without grain stand
upright in their arrogance and ignorance.*

~

One who knows others is considered clever, but one who knows himself is considered enlightened.

~

We gain more knowledge from failures than from success.

~

Advice given at the right time is better than gold given at the wrong time.

~

One who has traveled the road knows where the holes are deep.

~

Curiosity always finds knowledge.

~

To make steel pure, one must refine a hundred times.

Only through consistent practice can one become a master.

~

It takes a hundred years to train a person.

A trained person is very valuable. Although learning never stops, a person who has more experience is ahead of others.

Leadership

A great general need not blow his own trumpet.

~

One who is fit to sit facing the south.

Only a ruler or leader was considered worthy enough to sit facing south, which is the most favorable direction.

~

One looks up at a worthy person as one looks up to a mountain.

~

Do not intimidate. Empower.

~

If there is a strong general there will be no weak soldiers.

A good leader will know how to assess, train, and use people to their full potential.

~

One who is able to pull a strand of silk from a tangled mass.

A person who is able to restore order to a complicated mess.

~

One who is wise in strategy carries an army in his mind.

~

Without oars, a boat drifts.

~

One should not abuse authority. To go beyond is as wrong as to fall short.

~

When the emperor makes a mistake, all the people suffer.

~

It does not matter if the cat is black or white, so long as it catches mice.

This saying—meaning that the end justifies the means—is attributed to Deng Xiaoping, who used it to respond to criticism of his leadership.

~

Maintain soldiers a thousand days, use them for the moment.

Great leadership is as much about preparation as it is about action.

To be able to act swiftly, one must plan well in advance.

~

One who has conquered himself is worthy of leadership.

~

"Try" is a word of courage, but "can" is a word of power.

生活

劉克昌

Livelihood

Livelihood

Do not become a monk or a nun so late in life.

*A proverb that dissuades people from changing their
professions or doing things that they have not been
trained for.*

~

Do not be a frog sitting at the bottom of a well.

Do not limit yourself to a narrow perspective.

~

To be as uncomfortable as sitting on a
rug of needles.

To be in an unbearable situation, filled with anxiety.

~

Having to watch the eyebrows and countenance of another.

This means that one is in a servile position and must wait upon another or be at the mercy of a superior.

~

Better to learn one thing well than to know ten superficially.

~

To earn a living, a man must depend on his environment.

~

One who may be easy to serve yet difficult to please.

This describes a person who is always unhappy but never forthright, and one who is difficult to work for.

~

Exit the door, check the weather; enter the door, check the face.

This is an old saying that states that before leaving home, you should look outside to check the weather. But when you return home, to know the state of the house you must look inside at the occupant's face to see if he or she is in a happy or unhappy mood.

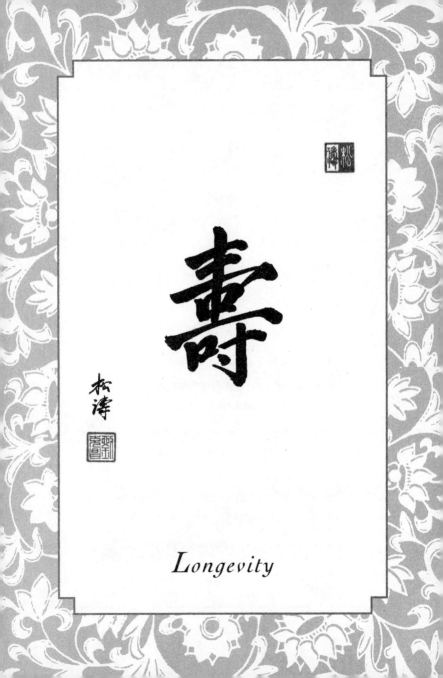

壽

Longevity

Longevity

Live healthy!
Live happy!
Live long!

~

May you live as long as the southern
mountain and enjoy happiness as bountiful
as the eastern sea.

The traditional Chinese wish for longevity is always combined with
happiness because a long life without happiness is a burden.

~

The leaves of the tree are many, but the root is one.
When the root is firm the branches flourish.

A good foundation guarantees success and longevity.

~

Write in the sand the bad things done to you.
Carve in stone the good things you
want to remember.

~

Even the weakest ink lasts longer than the
strongest memory.

~

The young and the bold favor speed, while
the old and the experienced move slowly.

*The young often lack the patience and care of the
old and wise.*

~

Good health is one blessing that cannot
be bought.

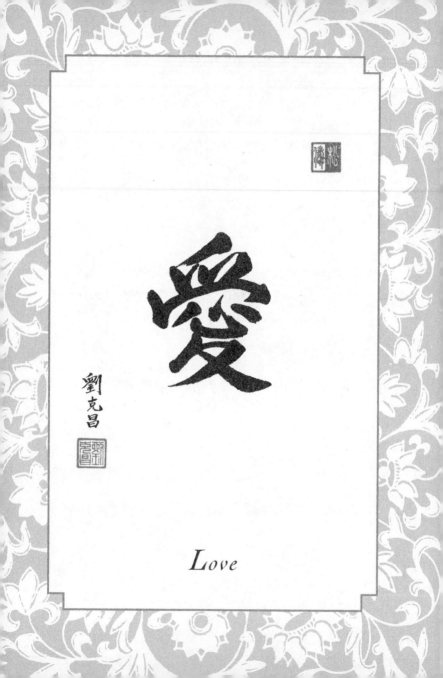

愛

劉克昌

Love

Love

Love as rare as twin lotuses on a single stalk.

A symbolic analogy of a happy and devoted couple.

~

A couple who spends one happy day together is
blessed with a hundred days of affection.

~

To love is to remember. One who is not
forgotten is not dead.

~

Great love makes us capable of great courage.

~

No journey is ever long with good company.

~

Love shows affection as naturally as a
sunflower faces the sun.

~

Love for a person must extend to the crows
on his roof.

*One's love for others must include acceptance of
their faults and imperfections.*

~

Love does not observe the passing of time.

~

Grow together with gray hair.

*A common wish for couples to grow old together in
love and respect.*

~

It is better to lose a wager than to lose a good
friend.

~

Everyone can hear your song,
but only those who love you will hear your sigh.

~

Love will come together over a silver river
on a bridge of magpies.

In China, July 7 is a day to celebrate love. On this day, the Chinese celebrate the famous love story of a farm boy who fell in love with a beautiful weaver from heaven. The distance meant that they could meet only once a year. Every year, helpful magpies built a path for the lovers to travel and meet. No matter how impossible, true love always finds a way.

Misfortune

Misfortune conquers timid souls, while great minds subdue setbacks.

~

The poor are those without talents; the weak are those without aspirations.

~

The tiles are broken and the ice is melted.

A saying denoting that fame is dead and the glory is gone.

~

To be born under the post-horse star.

Refers to someone who has the misfortune of being born to a hardworking life like the busy post-horse that is always on the road.

~

Blessings come but one at a time, but misfortune
visits in multiples.

~

To sit on a cold bench; to have a cold stove.

To be in a job or position without prospects.

~

One does not drink poison to quench a thirst.

*To be destructive and impractical during difficult times —equal to
jumping from the frying pan into the fire.*

~

In the land of hope, there is no winter.

~

Illness can empty any purse.

Moderation

To live long and well, employ moderation.

~

If one eats less, one will taste more.

A small bite savored will produce more enjoyment.

~

To extend your life by a year, take one fewer
bite each meal.

~

Pleasure cannot be pursued to its limit, for
pleasure could also be a fountain of sorrow.

~

For peace to prevail, all truth cannot be
expressed all the time.

道德

劉克昌

Morality

Morality

It is better to be completely ignorant than to be ill taught.

~

Bad habits are difficult to correct. One cannot straighten a crooked branch.

~

One who is a slave to his senses cannot rein his will into submission.

~

Sending charcoal in the snow is better than adding flowers to a brocade.

This means that friends who flatter us when we are doing well are adding flowers to an already intricate and well-decorated fabric. True friends will bring "charcoal in the snow," or give us assistance in our hour of need.

~

Virtue never lives alone. It always finds good company.

Necessity

Experience is a comb that we receive just
when we are going bald.

*This expression is used when we are most impatient
because it feels as if the solution always comes at the
very last moment.*

~

The most timid soul is made bold by necessity.

~

Necessity brings strength and perseverance.

~

Necessity forces us to make poor bargains.

~

Judge not one who tries and fails, but one
who fails to try.

Neighbors

Anyone can buy a good house, but good neighbors are priceless.

~

A fallen tree will lean on its neighbor.

~

Better good neighbors that are near than relatives far away.

~

A little help is worth more than a load of sympathy.

Nepotism

If a family lives in harmony, all affairs
will prosper.

~

Your ten fingers will always curl inward.

*A common reference to nepotism: it is as natural
as one's fingers bending toward the palm.*

~

They are all badgers from the same mound.

*This refers to a clan or group of people who all think
and may even look alike. They tend to view outsiders
with suspicion because they are not from the
same family.*

Obstinacy

The obstinate person does not possess opinions:
they possess him.

~

Ivy must cling to the wall; porridge will
stick to the pot.

~

When a centipede dies on the wall, it does
not fall down.

*This refers to laws that are no longer useful, institutions
that have outlived their need, or stubborn bureaucrats
who cling to power.*

~

Do not look at others with the eyes of a dog.

This proverb, often used to chide those who talk down to people, should be used with caution. It is an insult to compare someone to a dog, and one should not make rude comments to a person of low rank.

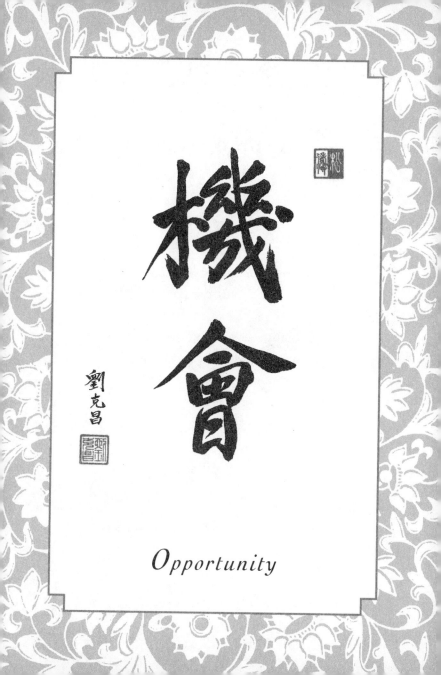

機會

劉克昌

Opportunity

Opportunity

One who gains mastery will create his own
opportunities.

~

An optimist sees an opportunity in every
calamity; a pessimist sees a calamity
in every opportunity.

~

Look upon adversity as opportunity in disguise.

~

Life can never give security; it can only promise
opportunity.

~

Opportunity is like catching the sun's rays.

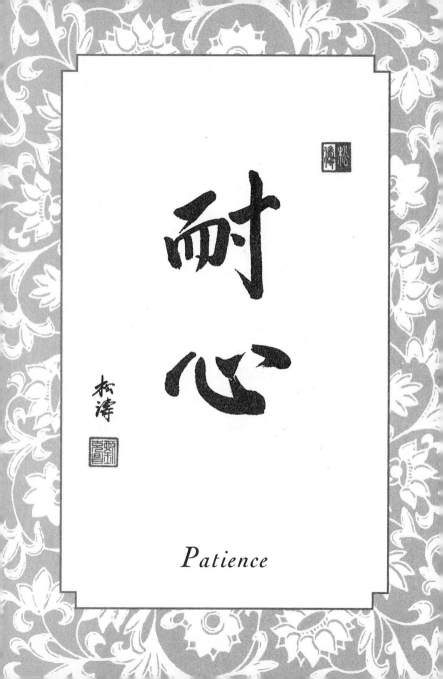

耐心

松濤

Patience

Patience

Patience is a tree with bitter roots that
bears sweet fruit.

~

Patience is wisdom in waiting.

~

Do not pull the seedlings to help them
grow faster.

*This advises patience and warns against
unnecessary meddling.*

~

Order moves slowly, but surely; disorder is
always in a hurry.

~

Inspiration comes from patience and perspiration.

~

A bird cannot fly until its feathers are
fully grown.

*Have patience. Do not attempt to do something
until you are ready.*

~

Fools who are in a hurry drink with chopsticks.

Impatience can bring illogical decisions.

~

In a struggle between strength and patience,
patience will win.

~

The best advice is often found on our pillows.

~

Patience is a virtue one must carry when traveling.

Peace/Good Wishes

One who is happiest finds peace and
harmony at home.

~

The seasons will return; all things are renewed.

Difficulties will pass and all will be well again.

~

Peace comes only when reason rules.

~

There are many paths to the top of the mountain.
Once there, you will find that the view is the same.

~

A guilty conscience is the enemy within.

~

He who knows the truth can die content.

~

Laws are useless when men are pure and are unenforceable when men are corrupt.

~

May a happy star always light your path.

~

May it always be spring with you.

In China, spring is a time of joy and celebration.

~

A kind word is worth a cold winter.

The gift of supportive comments can be a great comfort through difficult times.

~

The individual is the only one who can rescue his own spirit.

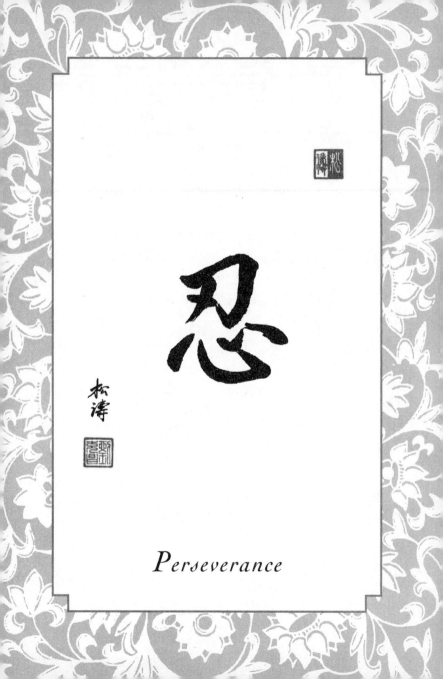

Perseverance

Perseverance

Even the tallest tower started from the ground.

~

Gems are polished by rubbing, just as men are
made brilliant by trials.

~

Perseverance is the water that wears away the
stone.

~

Experience is not a kind teacher, but it is always a
truthful one.

~

Either do not begin or, having begun,
do not give up.

This is a strong statement for the Chinese. It is the equivalent of saying that a person is determined to take something to completion.

~

To abandon something halfway
is to fail completely.

~

Victory belongs to the most persevering.

~

Better to light a candle than to curse the darkness.

~

Man can live on hope. No other animal can.

~

To move a big mountain, begin by removing the
small stones.

Poverty

Poverty without complaint is hard, just as wealth
with arrogance is easy.

~

Wealth and obscurity cannot equal poverty and
fame.

~

Poverty teaches value; greed breeds discontent.

~

Those who thirst will drink in silence.

*People who have tasted poverty will
protect their livelihood.*

~

One who is discontent is already poor.

~

One who does not know when he has enough is poor indeed.

~

To burn one day's gathering of firewood on the same day.

This means to live from hand to mouth and to have nothing left over.

~

The contented man, though poor, is happy. The discontented man, though rich, is sad.

~

One who can promise nothing is a poor person.

Good character is a source of wealth. One who cannot be trusted is not rich.

Prejudice

If the wind blows from one direction, a tree will grow inclined.

A twisted or bent tree is a symbol of prejudice because it receives wind from only one side, just like a person who subscribes to a single point of view and is unable to understand the position of others.

~

Prejudice springs from ignorance.

~

What a child learns in the cradle he will take with him to the grave.

~

A child will behave as he has been taught.
Tolerance is one of the first lessons to be learned.

Pride

Pride is often used to cover a weakness.

~

Do not have your eyes growing on your forehead.

*Used to refer to people who are proud and often pretend
not to see others because they think these others are
beneath them.*

~

One's shadow grows larger than life when
admired by the light of the moon.

*A proverb that makes fun of a person who has an
inflated image of himself.*

~

Pride and prejudice are brothers.

利潤

Profit

Profit

To lose a sheep but gain an ox.

To lose something of lesser value and gain something of greater value.

~

To lose a halberd but gain a lance.

To lose and gain something of equal value.

~

Profit is always directly related to risk.

~

Great profit may come from humble circumstances.

~

Do not profit from the misfortune of others.

~

If there are no clouds, there will be no rain.

Success does not come without hardship.

~

One must lose a worm to catch a fish.

Responsibility

Responsibility is the price of leadership.

~

Food and fodder must precede troops and horses.

This means that on top of responsibility, one must do things in the proper order. This is the equivalent of putting the horse before the cart.

~

One servant cannot serve two masters.

Leadership must come from one person. An employee cannot report to two bosses and have a clear direction.

~

Promises offered in a storm are forgotten in the calm.

~

It is often the busiest person who
has time to spare.

~

One who promises too much will find it
difficult to make good his words.

~

There is no one to sweep a common hall.

When responsibilities are not clear, the work will go undone.

誠

意

松濤

Sincerity

Sincerity

Eloquence provides persuasion, but truth
brings sincerity.

~

To tell only half the truth is to give life to a new lie.

~

The thoughtful never need words to show sincerity.

~

Better a red face than a black heart.

*Honest persons blush when embarrassed, while ruthless
liars don't. One who has the best of intentions will blush.
To be described as one who has a black heart is a strong statement
in Chinese culture. A black heart has a core of evil.*

~

No one has yet found any substitute for honesty.

策略

克昌

Strategy

Strategy

In war, there can never be too much deception.

~

Beat the grass to frighten the snakes.

To flush out the enemy or to drive out the competition.

~

Do not make a rule only to fall foul of it.

This means to be trapped by one's own device.

~

Every portal is an entry as well as an exit.

~

Sit atop the mountain and watch the tigers fight.

*This saying refers to one who watches two opponents contend with
each other, hoping that both will be eliminated.*

~

Know your limitations: seek shelter
while you can.

~

To conquer one hundred times out of
one hundred, study yourself and your
opponent well.

*Evaluate the strengths and weakness of yourself
and your competitor. Only then can you choose
the right strategy.*

~

A fish not caught by a hook may be caught
by a net.

The creative strategist seeks out alternatives.

~

Wait long, strike fast!

*A strategy that advocates great patience combined
with quick decisiveness.*

~

Do not hit the fly that lands on the tiger's head.

Warns against having good intentions but bad timing.

~

Whenever the water rises, the boat
will rise, too.

*This is commonly used in Chinese politics. It describes
people who join the right party or associate themselves
with powerful politicians so that they can ride on
their coattails.*

~

The foolish wander while the wise travel.

Always act with the destination in mind.

~

Do not remain in the open when the enemy
is concealed.

~

If there is a wave there must be a wind.

*This means to understand the consequences of
one's action—cause and effect.*

~

Three simple shoemakers equal one brilliant strategist.

A famous saying attributed to the early third-century strategist and statesman Zhuge Liang, comparing the combined intelligence of three ordinary people to that of one of the greatest Chinese generals and strategists. This means that one should combine all resources no matter how insignificant they may appear.

~

To leap far, take a long run.

~

Borrow the east wind!

This is a reference to an important battle in the war classic "Romance of the Three Kingdoms." A general had only one chance to storm a fortress and all his ships had to depend on the east wind to make the surprise attack successful.

~

Use every step as your base.

A cautious strategy that relies on advancement through small achievements.

~

If one man guards a narrow pass, ten thousand cannot get through.

A strategically placed barrier can achieve the impossible.

~

If you want to buy anything, ask three merchants.

This is a Chinese business principle that one must always compare offers. This practice prevents a business from becoming vulnerable to one supplier.

~

Of the thirty-six stratagems, "running away" is the best one.

The "Thirty-six Stratagems" is a renowned Chinese treatise on the art of war. It is often said that the last one, which recommends running away, is probably the wisest of them all.

~

When one is prepared, difficulties do not come.

It is a common perception that when one is ready for all contingencies, they seldom arise.

~

Do not lift a rock only to drop it on your own foot.

Do not make changes just for the sake of change.
Things could get worse.

~

Monkeys must disperse once their tree falls.

To get rid of a group of people, remove their common
bond or leader and they will disperse.

~

To force the untrained into battle is to waste
your troops.

A Confucian saying that advises against being
unprepared or squandering one's resources.

~

Kill the chicken to frighten the monkey.

Sacrifice or punish the less important as a warning or message to
the real culprit.

~

Occupy the higher ground to attain dominance.

A strong vantage point in combat has the most power because it
offers the most information.

~

The best tacticians are never impulsive; the best
leaders are never arrogant.

~

Spectators often have a better view than the
protagonists do.

*People who are too close to their problems may not
see the whole picture as impartial observers do.*

~

Do not attempt to fix with a single bite.

*A usual retort to someone who gives a simplistic solution to a
complex problem without understanding all the implications.*

~

When the snipe and the clam fight,
the fisherman benefits.

*A famous story tells of a bird whose bill was caught
in a pinching clam. The observing fisherman saw the
scuffle and was able to catch both. This teaches the
lesson that an observer can gain from the
quarreling of others.*

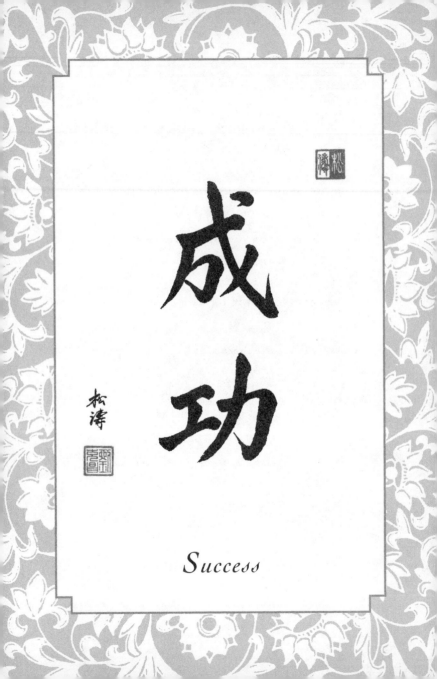

成功

Success

Success

True success comes from within. Do not hope to strengthen the weak by weakening the strong.

~

Ingenuity lights the path to success.

~

To climb a ladder you must start at the bottom.

~

Success as unstoppable as the path through split bamboo.

Although bamboo is strong, once it has been split, the break will be complete. This proverb refers to a winning streak that cannot be stopped.

~

Red so intense that it becomes purple.

This refers to a life-changing moment in one's career or reputation.
In an instant, a person can go from an unknown to a star.

~

Dress well and you will open all doors.

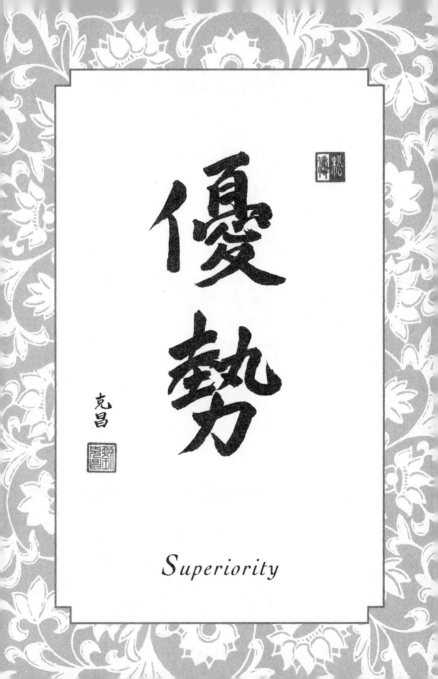

Superiority

Superiority

There are three marks of a superior person:
being virtuous, he is free from anxiety; being
wise, he is free from perplexity; being brave,
he is free from fear.

~

The mighty tree must catch the wind.

*The tree in this proverb refers to rich, powerful, or
famous persons who suffer controversy, lawsuits,
or unwanted publicity because of their high profile.*

~

One who oppresses others is always a coward.

~

The foolish will confuse power with greatness.

Suspicion

If you are standing upright, do not be concerned
if your shadow is crooked.

~

Suspicion will chase the wind and clutch at
shadows. A suspicious heart cannot find peace.

~

To the fearful, the reflection of a bow is that
of a snake.

This means that, when frightened and suspicious,
we see the reflection of an enemy or something sinister
in ordinary things.

Talent

One who wastes talent throws away his blessings.

~

Concealed talents benefit no one.

~

Just as incense emits no fragrance until it is burned, talent is not recognized until it is used.

~

Water can either float or sink a boat. Its fate is in the hands of the one who sails it.

~

A poor workman should not blame his tools.

Talent comes from within and is undeniable when shown.

Thought

Great thoughts can become great deeds.

~

With our thoughts we must build our world.

*A saying attributed to Buddha that our minds
shape the world we live in.*

~

Learning without thought is opportunity lost.

*To be a good student, one must be present in both mind
and body.*

Trust

All good relationships are rooted in trust.

~

When there is trust, no proof is necessary.

~

To be trusted is to be loved.

~

Promises offered in a storm are forgotten
in the calm.

Trust is to depend on someone through thick and thin.

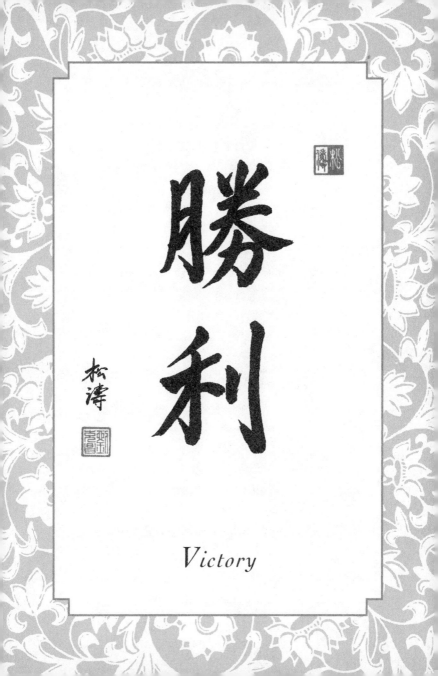

勝利

Victory

Victory

Fight only when you can win; move away when you cannot.

~

Avoiding conflict is also a victory.

~

To travel a thousand miles in one day.

A common saying that means to make great progress in a short period of time.

~

Greatness comes only when fame does not outshine truth.

~

Success and fortune will follow the brave.

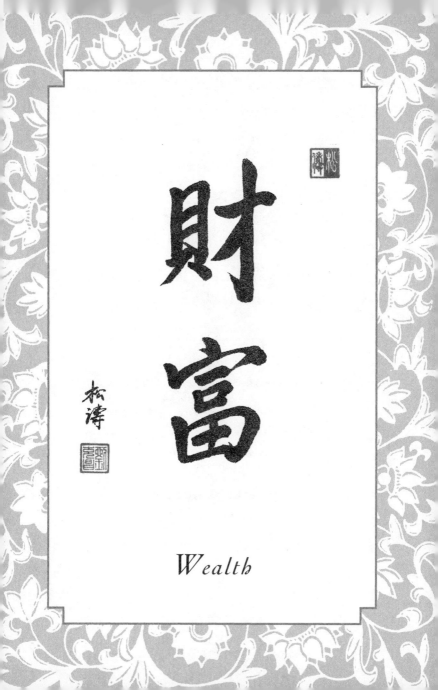

财富

Wealth

Wealth

Wealth, when used, is depleted. Learning,
when used, grows.

~

What is scarce is valued, what is plentiful is not.

~

One courts misfortune by flaunting wealth.

*Remember that there is always someone who
will trade places with a successful person when
given the opportunity.*

~

There is no wealth above a healthy body
and a happy heart.

~

If a man has no enemies, fortune has ignored him.

~

One who starts out to seek contentment finds great wealth.

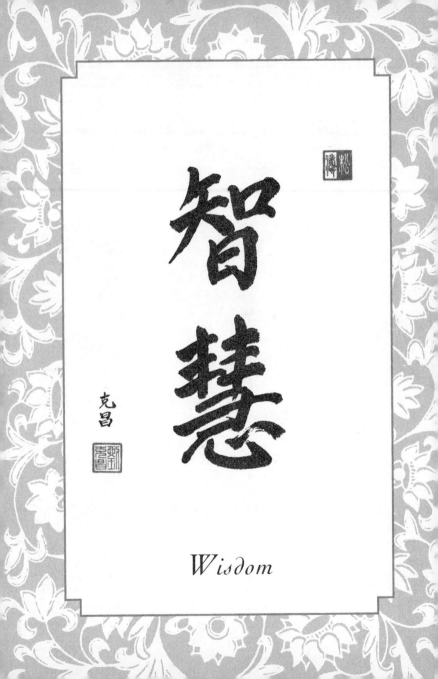

智慧

Wisdom

Wisdom

In a crisis, people grow wisdom.

~

Intelligence is endowed, but wisdom is learned.

~

Wisdom is attained by learning when to hold
one's tongue.

~

One who knows the most will speak the last.

~

Wise men may be learned. Learned men may
not be wise.

~

One who is wise enough to secure the good of
others has secured his own.

~

One word to the wise is sufficient.

~

A wise person knows when to play the fool.

~

We grow old fast. We grow wise slowly.

~

Discretion is the trusted friend of wisdom. A wise head must possess a closed mouth.

~

It takes a tree ten years to mature; it takes a man one hundred years to form.

Maturity and wisdom take a lifetime to achieve.

~

Learn as if life is one continuous lesson.

~

Youth can look only forward, but age can also look back.

~

It is easy to blame our memory when our judgment is at fault.

~

A silent fool can pass for a wise man.

The wise know when to remain silent and when to make their point known.

~

Silence is the trusted friend of wisdom.

Worry

The body's pain can be controlled, but that
of the mind cannot.

~

Worry never thwarted destiny.

~

Do not fret when the birds of worry fly over your
head; but when they stop to build nests, this
you must prevent.

~

Doubt can be more cruel than reality.

About the Authors

Theodora Lau is the author of *The Handbook of Chinese Horoscopes*, *The Chinese Horoscopes Guide to Relationships*, and *Chinese Horoscopes for Your Child*. Since the publication of her first book in 1979, Theodora's books have been translated into more than 17 languages and have introduced many topics of Chinese culture to readers all over the world. She was born in Shanghai and later moved to Southern California with her husband, Kenneth.

Kenneth Lau is an author, calligrapher, and illustrator whose work has been featured in *The Handbook of Chinese Horoscopes*, *The Chinese Horoscopes Guide to Relationships*, and *Chinese Horoscopes for Your Child*. Born in Shanghai, Kenneth is fluent in multiple Chinese dialects and skilled in a variety of Chinese calligraphy styles. After living in

Asia, Kenneth and Theodora have made Southern California their home for the past 25 years.

Laura Lau is a writer whose work has been featured in *Chinese Horoscopes for Your Child*. The daughter of Kenneth and Theodora Lau, Laura is a second-generation author on Chinese culture and horoscopes. *Best-Loved Chinese Proverbs* is her first book. Born in Hong Kong, she lives in Southern California with her husband, Harsh.